TRAVEL WITH THE GREAT EXPLORERS

Explore with

Francisco Pizarro

Lisa Dalrymple

Crabtree Publishing Company

www.crabtreebooks.com

Crabtree Publishing Company
www.crabtreebooks.com

Author: Lisa Dalrymple
Publishing plan research and development: Reagan Miller
Managing Editor: Tim Cooke
Designer: Lynne Lennon
Picture Manager: Sophie Mortimer
Design Manager: Keith Davis
Editorial Director: Lindsey Lowe
Editor: Kelly Spence
Proofreader: Kathy Middleton
Children's Publisher: Anne O'Daly
Production coordinator and prepress technician: Tammy McGarr
Print coordinator: Margaret Amy Salter

Produced by Brown Bear Books for
Crabtree Publishing Company

Photographs:
Front Cover: Getty Images: De Agostini Picture Library main;
Shutterstock: tr, cr, Steve Estvanik br;

Interior: Alamy: Glasshouse Images 10r, Independent Pictures Service 26b, Carlos Mora 6bl, North Wind Picture Archives 4–5t, 18t, 29l, Pictorial Press Ltd 20; **Architect of the Capitol:** 11tr; **Bibliografia Digital del Archivo historico del Guayas (AHG):** 10bl; **Bridgeman Art Library:** De Agostini Picture Library 27t, Giraudon 28; **Getty Images:** Hulton Archive 29br; **Historia General de las Indias:** Francisco Lopez de Gomara 25b; **Library of Congress:** 27b; **Shutterstock:** 23t, Roger Cuel 5b, Steve Estvanik 17t, Everett Historical 11b, 16b, Eric Isselée 24b, Carlos Santa Maria 21tr, Mark Skalny 23b, Christian Vinces 7t, Worldpics 24t; **Thinkstock:** 29tr, Maciej Bledowski 19l; Rafal Cichawa 6t, Judy Dillon 23cr, Dorling Kindersley 4–5, Fuse 22b, John Garcia Aunion 12t, Hemera 7b, istockphoto 16l, Robert Lerich 25cr, Jeroen Peys 13tr, stockphoto 7cr, Arne Thaysen 22t; **Topfoto:** British Library Board 17b, 20–21b, The Granger Collection 4l, 13b, 14, 19b, 26r, Topham Picturepoint 12b, World History Archive 18b.
All other artwork and maps, Brown Bear Books.

Brown Bear Books has made every attempt to contact the copyright holder. If you have any information please contact licensing@brownbearbooks.co.uk

Library and Archives Canada Cataloguing in Publication

Dalrymple, Lisa, author
        Explore with Francisco Pizarro / Lisa Dalrymple.

(Travel with the great explorers)
Includes index.
Issued in print and electronic formats.
ISBN 978-0-7787-1700-3 (bound).--
ISBN 978-0-7787-1704-1 (paperback).--
ISBN 978-1-4271-7704-9 (pdf).--ISBN 978-1-4271-7700-1 (html)

        1. Pizarro, Francisco, approximately 1475-1541--Juvenile literature. 2. Explorers--Peru--Biography--Juvenile literature. 3. Explorers-- Spain--Biography--Juvenile literature. 4. Peru--Discovery and exploration--Spanish--Juvenile literature. I. Title. II. Series: Travel with the great explorers

F3442.P776D35 2015   j985'.02092   C2015-903202-4
                                                                      C2015-903203-2

Library of Congress Cataloging-in-Publication Data

CIP available at the Library of Congress

Crabtree Publishing Company

www.crabtreebooks.com   1-800-387-7650

Printed in Canada/082015/BF20150630

Published in Canada
Crabtree Publishing
616 Welland Ave.
St. Catharines, ON
L2M 5V6

Published in the United States
Crabtree Publishing
PMB 59051
350 Fifth Avenue, 59th Floor
New York, New York 10118

Published in the United Kingdom
Crabtree Publishing
Maritime House
Basin Road North, Hove
BN41 1WR

Published in Australia
Crabtree Publishing
3 Charles Street
Coburg North
VIC, 3058

CONTENTS

Meet the Boss

In the 1500s, **Spanish** conquistador **Francisco Pizarro heard stories of incredible wealth in South America. Pizarro traveled to what is now Peru and overthrew the mighty Inca** empire—stealing land and riches.

JOINING UP

★Join the army—see the world!

Pizarro grew up and become a soldier. At that time, many soldiers were traveling to Spain's newly discovered territory in the **New World**. Some brought back treasure—if they survived. In 1502, Pizarro traveled to Hispaniola, an island in the Caribbean where Christopher Columbus had founded a **colony**. There, he joined an expedition headed for South America.

POOR BEGINNINGS

+ Explorer herds pigs as a child

+ Can't read or write

Francisco Pizarro was born in Spain sometime between 1470 and 1475. Born into **poverty**, he was the **illegitimate** son of a soldier. It is believed that Pizarro did not attend school and could not read and write. Instead, he working herding **boars**, or wild pigs.

Did you know?

Pizarro was distantly related to Hernán Cortés, the conqueror of the Aztec empire in Mexico. Stories of Cortés's success inspired Pizarro to set out to conquer the Inca empire in Peru.

My Explorer Journal

★ **If you were Pizarro urging your men to head to Peru, what might you say to convince them to cross the line in the sand and follow you?**

BETRAYAL!

★A deadly friend

In the New World, Pizarro befriended another Spanish explorer named Vasco Núñez de Balboa (below). Pizarro was part of Balboa's expedition in 1513, which was the first to reach the Pacific Ocean. But Pizarro was more loyal to Spain than to his friend. When the Spanish governor of Central America suspected Balboa of planning a rebellion, Pizarro was sent to arrest him. Balboa was tried and beheaded.

GOLD, GLORIOUS GOLD!

+ Stories encourage explorer's greed

Pizarro had heard that Hernán Cortés had conquered the Aztecs in Mexico and had discovered a city full of gold, silver, and other valuable goods—the capital, Tenochtitlán. Pizarro had also heard stories about the wealth of the Inca empire of Peru. The fortune hunter set out to find Peru and conquer the Inca.

LINE IN THE SAND

☛ Follow me—or buzz off!

Pizarro was an ambitious and ruthless leader. In 1526, while trying to reach Peru, the conquistador and his men were stuck on a beach in Colombia and short on supplies. Some men wanted to turn back. Pizarro drew a line in the sand. He pointed south and said to his men, "This is the way to Peru and its riches." Pointing north, he said, "That way is Panama and poverty." Thirteen men crossed the line to follow Pizarro to Peru.

Where Are We Heading?

FAILURE!

Pizarro first tried to reach Peru in 1524. He sailed south as far as Colombia before bad weather and lack of food forced him to turn back to Panama.

Pizarro was an experienced explorer when he set out to find the Inca empire. After one unsuccessful trip, he met the Inca on the very edge of Peru. Four years later, Pizarro returned to overthrow their empire.

THROUGH THE JUNGLE

☛ A new ocean

Early in his time in Central America, Pizarro lived for three years in Darién, a settlement founded by Balboa on the coast of what is now Colombia. In 1513, Pizarro trekked with Balboa west through the jungles of the **isthmus** of Panama. As they crossed the mountains in the middle of the isthmus, they became the first Europeans to see the Pacific Ocean.

FIRST CONTACT

+ Tumbez welcomes strangers

+ Pizarro plots its overthrow

In 1528, Pizarro met the Inca for the first time in the town of Tumbez in the northwest of what is now Peru. He found enough gold there to convince him that the stories of Inca treasure were true. Pizarro pretended to be friendly but left to get more support for an attack. When he returned four years later, Tumbez had been destroyed by civil war and disease. Pizarro kept searching for the heart of the Inca empire.

SUMMER CAPITAL
★ **Resort in the mountains**

★ **Spaniards interrupt ruler's stay**

Cajamarca was an Inca city in the Andes mountains, 470 miles (755 km) from Tumbez. The Inca rulers used it as the capital during the summer. It had hot springs where the ruler and his family bathed. When Pizarro and his men arrived in Cajamarca in November 1532, they **massacred** thousands of Inca warriors and took the Inca emperor Atahuallpa prisoner.

> "Great stranger, I am here with a request from my sovereign that you honor him with your presence at his camp near Cajamarca."
> *Inca messenger to Pizarro, November 1532*

HEART OF THE EMPIRE
+ **Capital in the mountains**

The Inca capital, Cuzco, lay among the high peaks of the Andes mountains. The region suffered from earthquakes, but Cuzco's buildings were constructed from huge blocks of stone that locked together to become earthquake-proof. The Inca believed gold was sacred and used it to cover the walls of their temples. Pizarro's men described buildings that looked like they had been dipped in gold.

A NEW CAPITAL
★ **Pizarro chooses site**

Pizarro founded a new Spanish capital in Peru in 1535, near the Pacific coast. He placed the first building block himself. The city is now known as Lima and is the capital of Peru. Pizarro believed founding the city was his most important achievement.

PIZARRO'S EXPEDITIONS TO PERU

Pizarro failed twice to reach the heart of the Inca empire. On his third trip, he captured the emperor, conquered the capital at Cuzco, and began to build a new Spanish capital at Lima.

Gallo Island

In 1526, on his second attempt to reach Peru, Pizarro and his men were stuck on Gallo Island off the coast of modern-day Colombia. The men were weak and hungry. When the governor of Panama sent a ship to rescue them, Pizarro drew a line in the sand and challenged his men to stay with him to find Peru. Thirteen men crossed the line to continue the expedition.

Tumbez

Pizarro reached the city of Tumbez in 1528. It was his first contact with the Inca empire. Convinced that Peru was full of riches, Pizarro hurried to Spain to get royal permission to explore farther. However, when he returned four years later, he found the city devastated by disease and warfare.

San Miguel

On his third expedition, Pizarro founded the first Spanish settlement in Peru in 1532, and built a fort, a cathedral, and a storehouse.

Panama City

Gallo Island

Tumbez

San Miguel

Cajamarca

Lima

Cuzco

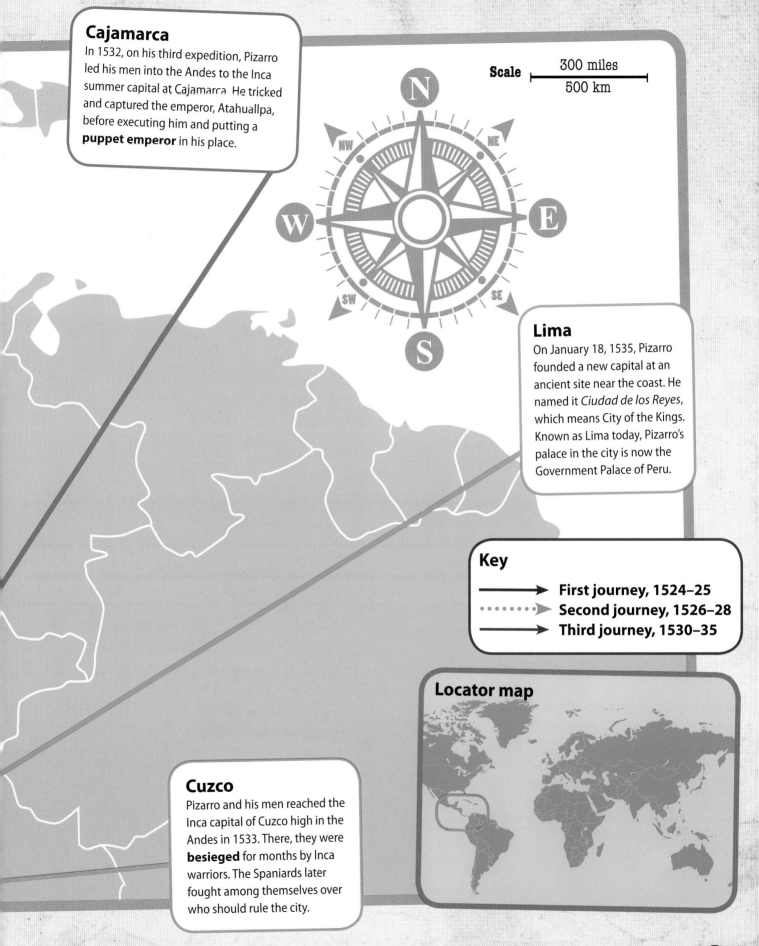

Cajamarca

In 1532, on his third expedition, Pizarro led his men into the Andes to the Inca summer capital at Cajamarca. He tricked and captured the emperor, Atahuallpa, before executing him and putting a **puppet emperor** in his place.

Scale 300 miles / 500 km

Lima

On January 18, 1535, Pizarro founded a new capital at an ancient site near the coast. He named it *Ciudad de los Reyes*, which means City of the Kings. Known as Lima today, Pizarro's palace in the city is now the Government Palace of Peru.

Key

→ **First journey, 1524–25**
·····► **Second journey, 1526–28**
→ **Third journey, 1530–35**

Locator map

Cuzco

Pizarro and his men reached the Inca capital of Cuzco high in the Andes in 1533. There, they were **besieged** for months by Inca warriors. The Spaniards later fought among themselves over who should rule the city.

Meet the Crew

Most of the men who traveled with Pizarro were poor Spanish soldiers, like himself. Some only traveled with him for a short time; others shared many of Pizarro's adventures.

KEEP IT IN THE FAMILY

★ **Pizarros strike it rich**

Pizarro had four half brothers who joined him on his final expedition to Peru. After their victory over the Inca, Francisco gave Hernando, Juan, and Gonzalo Pizarro important positions in running the Spanish **Viceroyalty** of Peru. Pizarro's other half brother was named Francisco Martín de Alcántara. He lived in Lima and helped raise Pizarro's three sons and one daughter along with his own children.

PIZARRO'S PARTNER

+ **Almagro misses out on riches**

The Spanish soldier Diego de Almagro was Pizarro's partner in the discovery of Peru. He stuck by Pizarro, even after losing an eye fighting native peoples. The two men worked together for decades. Pizarro usually led their expeditions. Almagro often stayed behind to find men and supplies. After they defeated the Inca, however, Pizarro and Almagro argued over who should govern Cuzco. In 1538, Hernando Pizarro had Almagro executed.

THE CONQUISTADORS

★ Spain's overseas conquerors

★ Pizarro one of golden generation

Many conquistadors helped build a Spanish empire in the New World. Pizarro traveled with many famous conquistadors, such as his friend Balboa. Others included Francisco de Orellana, who sailed down the Amazon River. Sebastián de Belalcázar conquered Nicaragua and Ecuador. Hernando de Soto (right) explored what is now the southern United States, including Florida, and was the first European to find the Mississippi River.

Did you know?

Pizarro and Almagro planned the conquest of Peru with a Spanish priest named Hernando de Luque. Luque raised money for the expeditions. He died in Panama in 1532.

CHARLES AND ISABELLA

☛ Conquistadors need consent

☛ Monarchs take share of loot

Conquistadors needed to ask their king for permission to conquer a new land. In 1528, after he had met the Inca in Tumbez, Pizarro sailed back to Spain to ask King Charles V for permission to conquer Peru. The King was away, so Queen Isabella signed an agreement stating that Pizarro was the only person allowed to conquer and govern Peru. In return, Pizarro had to send one fifth of any treasure he found back to the monarchs in Spain.

Check Out the Ride

The Spaniards traveled to Peru by ship, on foot, and on horseback. They discovered that the Inca had ships of their own and that Inca nobles were carried by servants.

Horses!

The Inca had never seen horses, which did not yet live in the Americas. They were terrified by Pizarro's 62 horses. The Inca warriors did not know how to fight the men riding on horseback.

TRAVEL UPDATE

Ideal Ships for Explorers

★If you're exploring along a coast, as Pizarro did when he sailed south from Central America to find Peru, try taking a **caravel**. Caravels were small, light ships. They could sail along the coast or travel up rivers. They could also carry plenty of food, weapons, and horses. But the tiny ships were cramped. The passengers and crew slept in hammocks below deck.

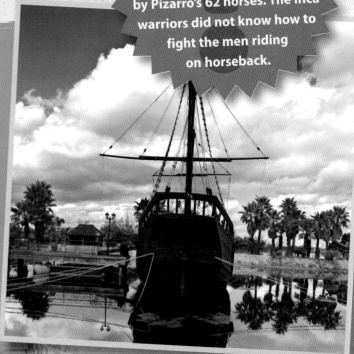

REMARKABLE RAFT

☞ Pilot spots Inca vessel

Bartolomé Ruiz, who sailed Pizarro's ships, once spotted a huge wooden raft. It was powered by a sail and had a shelter built on the deck. This was a **balsa**—a raft the Inca used for ocean-going voyages. Ruiz reported that the balsa he saw was loaded with gold cups and plates, silver mirrors, fine cloth, rubies, and crowns! No wonder the Spaniards were so eager to find the Inca treasure.

INGENIOUS INCA

★ **Roads in the mountains**

★ **Bridges not for fainthearted!**

Much Inca territory lay high in the mountains. The Inca built roads over steep passes to connect different parts of their empire. Only royal messengers were allowed to use the roads. The roads zigzagged back and forth to climb steep slopes or went up long flights of stone steps. In order to cross ravines, they built **suspension bridges** from rope. The bridges swayed and wobbled as people crossed them. There was often a deep drop beneath them.

DON'T DROP THE LITTER

☛ **Rulers ride on subjects' shoulders**

Inca nobles were carried around on special **litters**, which were platforms supported between two long poles. Servants carried the litters on their shoulders. The poles were decorated with silver, animal-shaped heads on the ends. The most luxurious litters had a seat covered with pillows, surrounded by walls of cloth, and a roof made of beautiful feathers. Some Spaniards began using litters to get around, forcing the Inca people to carry them.

Solve It With Science

Inca Arms

Inca warriors fought with spears, clubs, and bows and arrows. They also used weighted strings called bolas. When a bola was thrown, it became tangled around the enemy.

Advanced technology helped the Spanish conquer Peru—but the Inca had their own innovative science, too, which helped them solve problems in their daily lives.

BANG! BANG! BANG!

- ☞ Weapons fire invisible missiles
- ☞ Guns give Spaniards the edge

European soldiers began using gunpowder weapons in the late 1400s. The Spaniards in Peru used a long-barreled gun called an arquebus, and small cannons called falconets. These weapons terrified the Inca, who fought with spears and swords. The Inca called the European weapons "thunder from heaven." They thought the guns must fire invisible darts. The Inca's confusion gave the Spanish an advantage in battle.

TRAVEL UPDATE

Let's figure this out

★ On a voyage, try using an **astrolabe** to measure the height of the Sun above the horizon. This allows you to work out your **longitude**, or north or south position. If it's cloudy, try **dead reckoning**. Take notes of the time, the ship's direction, and its speed to help you figure out how far you have traveled.

Did you know?

Pizarro was accompanied by an expert navigator named Bartolomé Ruiz. His job was to sail Pizarro's ships to Peru.

CLIMATE CONTROL

The Inca grew crops on terraces—ledges cut into mountainsides. They discovered that crops grew differently in different places. To study this, they carved the land at a site called Moray into bowl shapes using rings of terraces. Each bowl got different amounts of sun, shade, and heat. The Inca studied the different models to figure out where it was best to grow corn and potatoes in the mountains.

INCA BUILDING

+ Explorer to take scientific log

Inca cities were surrounded by huge walls built with stones that weighed up to 15 tons (13.6 metric tons). The Inca carved and fit the stones together perfectly without needing cement. Doorways were built in a **trapezoid** shape. The shape acted like an archway, giving walls extra support so they could withstand earthquakes.

FAB FOODIES

★ **Fancy a year-old potato?**

★ **Do you want salt with that?**

The Inca had learned how to **preserve** food to store it for the winter. They freeze-dried potatoes to create *chuño*, which kept for over a year. The Inca also used salt to preserve food. Near Maras, a saltwater spring runs out from a mountain. The Inca directed the water into pools on terraces. When the water evaporated, the Inca harvested the crust of salt that was left behind.

Hanging at Home

In Peru, Pizarro and his men visited Inca towns where they stayed in comfort. They also began to build their own towns. At other times, they weren't so lucky.

STRANDED!

★ **Explorers face enemies, sickness, hunger**

★ **Things can only get better!**

On their first two attempts to conquer Peru, the explorers were attacked by natives and jungle animals. They also suffered from new diseases which their bodies had no defenses against. Starvation was common. At Hungry Harbor, Pizarro's stranded men ate shellfish, snakes, and seaweed. They even boiled leather to eat!

HOME FROM HOME

☞ **Explorers build European town in Peru**

☞ **Watch out for pests!**

Pizarro first visited Tumbez in 1528. When he returned in 1532, he found the population had been wiped out by **smallpox**, a disease introduced by the Spaniards. Pizarro built a new town called San Miguel. Similar to towns in Spain, it had a fortress, a city hall, a storehouse, and a church, where Pizarro erected a cross. The first church service celebrated in South America was held here. The climate was warm and dry—but the Spaniards complained about snakes and spiders. The Spaniards used slaves to **quarry** the stone to build the town.

PALACES FOR EVERYONE!

+ Inca capital taken over

After Pizarro's men defeated the Inca, they moved into the capital at Cuzco. It was the wealthiest city they had ever seen. While Hernando Pizarro took treasure back to King Charles V in Spain, his brothers and Almagro each built their own palaces. (Hernando built his own when he returned.) The Spaniards built their palaces and a cathedral on top of the strong Inca walls.

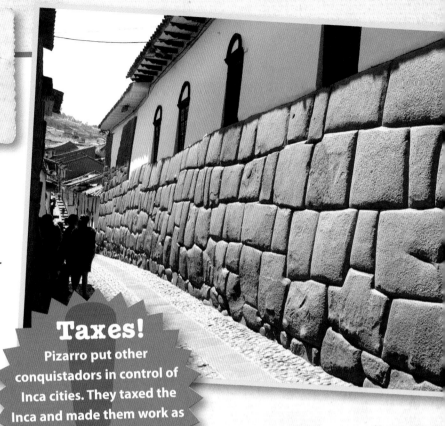

Taxes!

Pizarro put other conquistadors in control of Inca cities. They taxed the Inca and made them work as slaves. The Spaniards became very rich.

LIFE OF LEISURE

★ **Put your feet up!**

★ **Conquistador enjoys retirement**

Pizarro built a new capital city closer to the coast. It was easier to reach by sea. Today, it is called Lima. Here, Pizarro lived quietly with his family—his wife, who was an Inca princess, and their two children. He was looked after by Inca servants. Pizarro spent his time playing *pelota*, which is a game similar to handball, or playing cards and gambling. But if any of Pizarro's brothers reported trouble in the empire, he put on his armor and went off to lead the fight—although sometimes he sent others.

Meet the Inca

In only a few centuries, the Inca had built a huge empire that stretched from the Amazon rain forest through Colombia, Ecuador, Peru, Bolivia, Chile, and Argentina.

FALL OF THE EMPIRE

☞ **Killed by sickness**

When Pizarro first arrived on the coast of Peru, the ruler of the Inca was named Huayna Capac. The Inca believed their emperors were descended from the gods. But Huayna Capac died in 1527 from smallpox. The native peoples had no **immunity** to the European disease.

INCA CIVIL WAR

+ **Brother against brother**

+ **Tragic consequences**

After the death of Huayna Capac, his sons Huáscar and Atahuallpa went to war over the throne. This was the War of the Two Brothers, which broke out in 1529. In 1532, Atahuallpa emerged victorious, but the war and the smallpox **epidemic** had left the Inca weakened. That was one of the reasons why just a few Spaniards were able to overthrow an entire empire.

My Explorer Journal

★ **Tell a story about your last vacation. Does it change a little each time you tell it? Pretend you are recording your story on a *quipu*. What events would you use as reminder knots?**

Weather Forecast

WRAP UP WARM!
The tallest peaks in the Andes are covered in snow all year long. The Inca believed spirits lived in the high mountains and in the sky. As sacrifices, the Inca dressed young children in their best clothes and led them up the mountains. The children were drugged, tied up, and left to die from the cold. These sacrifices were part of the Inca religion, which was based on the worship of the Sun and the Moon.

STRING THEORY

★ **Messages tied up in knots**

★ **Records remain a mystery**

The Inca kept records by tying knots in string. These records were called *quipu*. The size and position of the knots recorded numbers, events, or other information. Today no one knows what the quipu mean. Official messages were carried by *chaskis*. These runners sprinted along roads to the next runner, passing the message in a relay. When a message was sent from Cuzco to Cajamarca to tell Atahuallpa he had won the war against Huáscar, it only took five days. The message was passed between 300 runners!

Meeting and Greeting

Pizarro's first contact with the Inca in 1528 was friendly, although the Inca were suspicious of the Europeans. When Pizarro came back four years later, he only brought an army of 168 men.

AMBUSH

★ **Spaniards seize the Inca**

★ **Snatched right under his army's nose**

On November 16, 1532, Atahuallpa came to meet Pizarro in Cajamarca. Carried on a litter, he was surrounded by 6,000 warriors. The town square was empty except for a Spanish priest, who told Atahuallpa the Inca should become **Christians**. Instead, the emperor threw the priest's Bible on the ground. The meeting was a trick. Pizarro had hidden his men around the square with guns and cannons. The Spaniards opened fire killing hundreds of Inca warriors. Then, they rushed out and seized Atahuallpa, taking him prisoner.

HELD FOR RANSOM

+ A room of gold and silver...

... but the emperor still gets the chop!

Held prisoner, Atahuallpa offered Pizarro a roomful of treasure in exchange for his life. He gave him 13,000 pounds (6,000 kg) of gold and 26,000 pounds (11,800 kg) of silver. However, the Spaniards still put him on trial for murdering his brother, Huáscar, in the battle for the throne, and rebelling against the Spanish. Atahuallpa was found guilty and sentenced to death. He was hanged on July 26, 1533.

Did you know?

Pizarro did not really want to have Atahuallpa killed, but the soldiers of Diego de Almagro insisted that the emperor must die to prevent a further Inca revolt.

- ☞ First encounter fuels explorer's greed
- ☞ Gold and silver everywhere

When Pizarro visited Tumbez in 1528, he became convinced the Inca were very wealthy. He saw temples full of treasure, and ate food off gold and silver plates. The Inca called gold "the sweat of the Sun" and silver "the tears of the Moon." They used the precious metals to make offerings to their gods. Pizarro was overcome with greed and became obsessed with overthrowing the Inca empire.

PUPPET ON A STRING

★ Manco Inca has no power

Pizarro chose a half brother of Atahuallpa, Manco, as the new Inca emperor. He had to do what Pizarro told him, however. Eventually, Manco came to resent his lack of power. In 1536, he gathered an army and laid **siege** to the Spaniards in Cuzco. He trapped them inside the city for a year before retreating to the remote mountains.

TRAVEL UPDATE

Into the Mountains

★ What better way to enjoy Peru than a visit to the hot springs? In 1532, Pizarro visited Atahuallpa at Cajamarca, where hot water bubbled up from the ground in natural baths. Try a healthy **fast**, as Atahuallpa was doing when Spanish messengers arrived. But don't be tempted by the water—the springs are reserved for the emperor and his family only. Anyone else who takes a dip is put to death!

I Love Nature

In the rain forests of the Amazon and the high Andes mountains, Pizarro and his men saw plants and animals that no European had ever seen before.

IN THE RAIN FOREST

★ **Amazon is world's largest jungle**

★ **Full of dangerous creatures!**

Some of the Spanish men kept journals of their travels in the Inca empire. They wrote about parrots, monkeys, and giant anteaters living in the jungle of eastern Peru. They were scared by boa constrictors—snakes that squeeze their prey to death—and by crocodiles. They also would have been on the lookout for jaguars!

SACRED CATS

☛ **Puma power inspires Inca**

The Inca had great respect for large cats, particularly the puma and the jaguar. *Puma* is the Inca word for a mountain lion or cougar. Similar to the jaguar, the puma is a fearsome hunter that lives a solitary life. It can survive in many areas, from the high mountains to the coastal forests. To the Inca, this made the cats sacred symbols of strength and power.

DON'T GET THE HUMP

+ "Little camels" far from desert

Some of the strangest animals the Spaniards saw looked like woolly sheep with long necks. They thought the Inca were calling the animals "lamb." In fact, they were llamas, which the Spaniards called little camels. The Inca kept llamas to carry loads and to provide leather, manure for fuel, and meat. A smaller relative of the llama, the alpaca, provided fine wool.

AERIAL GIANT

★ Bird loves battlefields

Andean condors are some of the world's largest flying birds. A condor's wingspan can stretch over 10 feet 6 inches (320 cm) wide. It's head has very few feathers and stands out above the black body. The condor eats **carrion**, or dead flesh. Pizarro's men often saw them pecking at dead bodies left on the battlefield or soaring high in the sky on currents of air.

DON'T BE SO CORNY

☞ Inca live on highland staple

The most important crop for the Inca was corn, which they called maize. The Inca year was based on the seasons for planting corn in spring and harvesting it in the fall. Corn was ground into flour to make beer, as well as the flat bread, called tortilla, that was eaten at almost every meal. Corn was so important to the Inca they planted a "garden" of gold and silver corn cobs behind the Temple of the Sun in Cuzco.

Fortune Hunting

When Pizarro was a poor swineherd in Spain, he dreamed of becoming rich and receiving a title. When he heard stories about a land of gold called Peru, he was determined to find and conquer it.

DON'T SPEND IT ALL AT ONCE!

☛ King's ransom goes a long way

☛ Soldiers make a lifetime's money in one trip

In his effort to stay alive, Atahuallpa collected a roomful of gold and twice as much silver from throughout his kingdom to offer Pizarro. This was unimaginable wealth. Pizarro gave each of his soldiers 45 pounds (20 kg) of gold and 90 pounds (41 kg) of silver. The gold alone represented about 90 years' pay for a Spanish soldier or sailor. Pizarro's horsemen received double the amount!

MONARCH LOVES MONEY

+ Conquistadors head out...

+ ... treasure flows in!

When Pizarro was preparing to explore Peru in 1529, the explorer Hernán Cortés had just returned to Spain. He brought treasures from Mexico, including **obsidian**, turquoise, jade, silver, and gold, as well as some Aztec people, jaguars, an opossum, and an armadillo. Charles V received "the king's fifth," meaning 20 percent of all Cortés took from the Aztecs. The King encouraged Pizarro to do the same with the rich Inca.

RICH AND POWERFUL

★ **Explorer's dreams come true**

★ **Not bad for a pig herder**

When he shared the Inca gold, Pizarro kept 14 times as much for himself as he gave to his men. But financial wealth was not his only reward. King Charles V made Pizarro a nobleman and made him governor of the Spanish province of New Castile. Pizarro lived in a palace in Lima and finally had the riches and the title he had dreamed of.

THAT'S NOT FAIR!

☛ **Conquistador cut out of reward**

Diego de Almagro was not with Pizarro when the Spaniards captured Atahuallpa at Cajamarca in November 1532. He was in Panama, raising another army to go to Peru. When he returned, Pizarro did give him some money, but not a full share of Atahuallpa's gold and silver. Almagro's men were not happy. This was the beginning of many problems between Pizarro and Almagro.

My Explorer Journal

★ **Conquistadors sent reports to Spain to get their king to continue to fund their expeditions. The reports were called probanzas. The conquistadors listed what riches the king might gain from a new land—as well as mentioning their own bravery. Use evidence given on this page to write a probanza to persuade the king to support an expedition in Peru.**

Did you know?

In the 1500s and early 1600s, treasure flowing in from the New World made Spain the wealthiest and most powerful country in Europe.

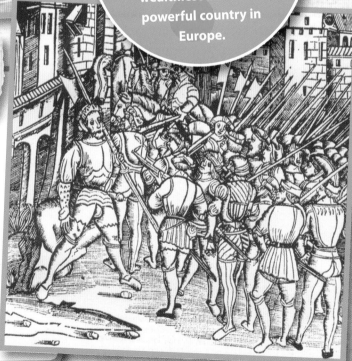

This Isn't What it Said in the Brochure!

Pizarro's men had the chance to earn riches beyond belief—but they also faced sickness, starvation, and danger. Most of them did not survive long enough to claim their rewards.

LIFE IS TOUGH

☞ **Young soldier faces long odds**

☞ **Gets taste of life in America**

In Hispaniola, the young Francisco Pizarro soon learned that being a conquistador was tough. In January 1510, he ended up defending a fort at San Sebastián, on the coast of what is now Colombia. The fort was attacked by native warriors. By the time help arrived, approximately 300 men were dead, either by poison arrows, starvation, or disease.

 **Weather Forecast**

HAVE YOU SEEN MY TOES?

Winters in the Andes are bitterly cold. On their march to Cajamarca in 1532, Pizarro and his men were so cold their shivering made their armor rattle. When Diego de Almagro led an army through the mountains to Chile in 1535, men's feet froze. When they pulled off their boots, their toes came off with them!

UNDER ATTACK!

+ **I thought you were on our side...**

+ **Puppet ruler cuts his strings**

In 1536, the Spaniards' chosen emperor, Manco, turned against them. He surrounded Cuzco with 200,000 warriors, trapping 196 Spaniards inside including Juan, Gonzalo, and Hernando Pizarro. The Inca used **slingshots** to fire stones wrapped in burning cotton into the city, which set the rooftops on fire. The Spaniards fought off the Inca for nearly a year, before Diego de Almagro's army arrived from Chile and the Inca retreated to the remote mountains.

Did you know?

The Europeans carried diseases such as smallpox, measles, typhus, cholera, and malaria. So many native people died from these diseases that the people of the Americas were changed forever.

WHO GETS CUZCO?

★ **Conquistadors quarrel**

★ **Tensions rise**

After ending the siege of Cuzco in 1536, Diego de Almagro claimed the city. He took Hernando and Gonzalo Pizarro prisoner. Juan had died during the siege. Francisco Pizarro sent an army to win Cuzco back, but Almagro defeated them on July 12, 1537. After Gonzalo Pizarro escaped, however, Almagro agreed to release Hernando in return for control of Cuzco. But tensions between the old comrades were reaching dangerous levels.

End of the Road

Pizarro defeated the Inca empire, but he would pay for many of his cruel actions against the people. He was not the only invader who met a horrible end.

Empire

The last Inca emperor, Túpac Amaru, reigned in Vilcabamba. He was captured and executed by the Spanish in September 1572, bringing a final end to the Inca empire.

BETRAYED!

- Cuzco costs Almagro dearly
- Old friend strangled to death

Pizarro's agreement to surrender Cuzco to Diego de Almagro in the summer of 1537 was a trick. Within a year, Pizarro sent an army from Lima to Cuzco. Almagro was sick at the time, and without his leadership, his followers—the *Almagristas*—were easily defeated. The Pizarros easily entered Cuzco. They captured Almagro, who was put on trial and executed by Hernando Pizarro on July 8, 1538.

DEATH OF THE CONQUEROR

- ★ Pizarro's last lunch
- ★ Almagristas get revenge

Three years after Almagro's death, a group of Almagristas took their revenge. On June 26, 1541, Francisco Pizarro was having lunch when the plotters burst in. They cornered Pizarro and stabbed him to death. They proclaimed Almagro's son governor of Peru, but he was defeated by forces loyal to Pizarro and was executed on September 16, 1542.

THIRD CASUALTY

+ Manco killed

After killing Pizarro, the Almagristas fled to Manco, the former emperor. He was living in Vilcabamba, a remote region in the Andes. Manco agreed to protect the plotters. Later, however, the Spaniards decided to prove their loyalty to the new governor of Peru. In 1544, they stabbed Manco to death during a game of horseshoes.

> **Close the door, Chavez, and bar it. Only give me time to get my armor on."**
> *Francisco Pizarro to a friend as the plotters entered his palace, June 26, 1541*

FAMILY FORTUNES

☛ Pizarro brothers get lucky (not!)

None of Francisco's brothers did very well out of the conquest of Peru. Juan Pizarro was killed in 1536, in the Inca attack on Cuzco. Hernando Pizarro spent 23 years in prison after executing Almagro. Francisco Martín de Alcántara was killed trying to defend Francisco from his **assassins**. Gonzalo Pizarro tried to take power from the Spanish governor of Peru. In 1548, he was captured and executed. His head was put on display in Lima as a warning to others.

GLOSSARY

Note: Some boldfaced words are defined where they appear in the book.

assassins People hired to murder someone else, often a political person

astrolabe A device used to measure the angle between the horizon and astronomical objects

balsa A large raft with a sail, used by the Inca for ocean-going voyages

carrion The decaying flesh of dead animals

Christians People who follow the teachings of Jesus Christ

colony A settlement founded in one country by another country

conquistador A Spanish soldier of fortune and conqueror in the New World

dead reckoning A method of navigation based on measuring a ship's speed and direction

empire A number of countries all controlled by the same ruler

epidemic A widespread outbreak of a disease

fast To go without food for a period of time

illegitimate Born to parents who were not married at the time

immunity The ability of a body to resist disease

isthmus A narrow strip of land that connects two large land masses

litters Covered beds or seats between two long poles and carried on people's shoulders

massacred Killed a large number of people violently and unnecessarily

navigator A person who directs travel by figuring out location, route, and distance traveled

New World North, Central, and South America

obsidian A dark volcanic glass formed when lava cools

poverty Lack of money or material possessions

preserve To treat food to stop it from going rotten

puppet emperor An emperor in name only, who rules on behalf of another

quarry To dig stone from the ground

siege A military action in which a force surrounds a place to force its surrender

slingshots Handheld catapults used to throw missiles

smallpox A deadly disease that causes a skin rash, fever, loss of memory, and confusion

suspension bridges Bridges that are hung from ropes or cables

trapezoid A four-sided shape with two parallel sides

viceroyalty A territory ruled over by a representative of a king or queen

Around 1475 or a little earlier, Pizarro is born in poverty in Trujillo, Spain.

September: Traveling with Vasco Nuñez de Balboa in Panama, Pizarro is one of the first Europeans to see the Pacific Ocean.

During a second expedition, Pizarro and his men are stranded on the island of Gallo; Pizarro draws a line in the sand and 13 soldiers cross it to go forward to Peru.

1475   1509   1513   1524   1527   1528

November: Pizarro sails from Spain to Hispaniola in the New World.

November: Pizarro and Almagro set out on their first attempt to find Peru.

April: Pizarro finally makes his first contact with the Inca at Tumbez.

ON THE WEB

www.ducksters.com/biography/explorers/francisco_pizarro.php
The story of Francisco Pizarro and his conquest of the Inca empire

www.pbs.org/opb/conquistadors/peru/peru.htm
A PBS site to on the Spanish conquistadors

www.biography.com/people/francisco-pizarro-9442295
A biography of Pizarro with a link to a short video (TV-PG)

http://incas.mrdonn.org/index.html
Information, games, and quizzes about the Inca empire for kids, with an Inca perspective on the arrival of Pizarro and the Spanish

BOOKS

DiConsiglio, John. *Francisco Pizarro: Destroyer of the Inca Empire* (Wicked History). Children's Press, 2008.

Hoogenboom, Lynn. *Francisco Pizarro: A Primary Source Biography*. PowerKids Press, 2006.

Somervil, Barbara A. *Empire of the Incas* (Great Empires of the Past). Chelsea House Publishers, 2010.

Sonneborn, Liz. *Pizarro: Conqueror of the Mighty Incas* (Great Explorers of the World). Enslow Publishers Inc, 2010.

Zronik, John. *Francisco Pizarro: Journeys through Peru and South America* (In the Footsteps of Explorers). Crabtree Publishing, 2005.

December: After visiting Spain to gain permission from the King to conquer Peru, Pizarro begins his third expedition.

November: Pizarro's men massacre the Inca at Cajamarca and take Atahuallpa prisoner before killing him.

February: Manco turns on the Spaniards and besieges Cuzco.

April: The Pizarros defeat Almagro and execute him on July 8.

June 26: Supporters of Almagro murder Pizarro in his palace in Lima.

1531 1532 1533 1535 1536 1537 1538 1541

May: Landing in Tumbez, Pizarro discovers the Inca empire is suffering from the results of smallpox and civil war.

November: Pizarro and his men capture the Inca capital of Cuzco.

January: Pizarro founds the City of the Kings, now Lima.

April: Almagro captures Cuzco, taking the Pizarro brothers captive. He agrees to release them in return for control of Cuzco.

INDEX